Exploring

your

potential

Who am I and
what am I doing here?

Julie Farha
Founder of Clear Insight, LLC

Exploring

your

potential

Who am I and
what am I doing here?

Julie Farha
Founder of Clear Insight, LLC

ISBN: 0-9793301-0-6
       978-0-9793301-0-0

Library of Congress: Pending

To order contact:
julie@clearinsightllc.com
www.clearinsightllc.com

Book Cover Design by The Cricket Contrast
Editor, Suzy Jimerson-Overholt, sumusic@aol.com

EVOLVING JOURNEYS PUBLISHING HOUSE
www.evolvingjourneys.com

Printed in the United States of America

Personal Growth

Contents

Dedication

For my grandmother, Sittie Marguerite, for always seeing who I truly am. Thank you for continuing to remind me of this even now that you are Home.
I miss your face.

Thanks

To my parents, George and Brenda Farha, for giving me the opportunity to explore who I truly am. You set the tone for my journey by demonstrating the value of generosity, integrity and being of service. I could not have done this without your love and support.

To my sisters, Gayle, Joan and Laura. You inspire me daily with your beauty, humor and dedication to others.

To all of my nieces, nephews, aunts, uncles and cousins. Thank you for the gift of family.

To my spiritual family. Thank you for being my teachers, for constantly pushing me to push myself and for helping me get unstuck when necessary.

To my friend, Gigi Strharsky. Thank you for being my cheerleader and for all that you and the ladies do for me.

To Zeus, my little dog with the huge spirit. Thank you for teaching me how to receive and for making me laugh so often. I am thankful every day that you are in my life.

To all of those who helped me with the book process including Suzy Jimerson-Overholt, my editor and friend. Thank you for your support and for believing in this book.

To Victoria Barna and Mary Dougherty for your guidance and support.

Finally, to quote my father, **"It's a great life!"**

x

Introduction

Many seek to better themselves and better their lives. I believe that each person's journey begins and ends with understanding more of who he or she is truly. It is the root of our existence. It is what guides us, inspires us and provides inner peace.

We all have similar issues, challenges and fears in life; yet, they may seem different in their outer appearances. Knowing more of who we truly are is the answer, no matter the question. When we know more of who we are, we release fears and pain and welcome and embrace the love and peace we all crave.

Each path to self-discovery is unique. This book is a tool designed to explore, inspire and reveal more of who you are. If you are beginning your path, this book will offer new insights and perspectives. If you have been on your path for quite some time, these tools are reminders of the basic foundation upon which you began your journey. As you read along, take what feels right to you into your heart and disregard the rest. From time to time, pick it up again to show yourself how far you've come on your journey.

I believe that learning who we are is why we are here. It is the most important journey and has the greatest rewards. It is my intention for this book to assist you along your journey and give you a glimpse of the amazing being that you are.

Enjoy!

Chapter 1

Who Am I and What Am I Doing Here?

"Let him who would move the world first move himself."

Socrates

When we think of who we are our thoughts go to places such as our profession, marital or financial status, religious or cultural affiliation. It is good to celebrate our differences, vocations, accomplishments and cultures. These are parts of the expression of who we are. It's important to honor these aspects of ourselves. However, they are not who we are but only expressions of our personalities.

Who you are and what you are doing here is a journey of discovering the light, love and power that you possess for that is who you truly are. We are all loving, gifted,

1

valuable and compassionate beings. However, we may not remember those aspects of ourselves. Exploring your potential is about understanding the depths and layers of yourself. It's about releasing the fears and negativities in order to reveal your gifts, truths, worth and compassion and to learn what matters to you. As you discover who you are you realize what you are doing here. You consciously craft a life that reflects your truth, your passions, your talents and creativity.

When you know who you are you have more confidence and less doubt, more love and less fear, more peace and less pain, more trust and less worry. It is an ongoing journey of self-discovery with many revelations along the way, revelations that create the picture of you and the luminous aspects of you.

There are five areas that hold clues to who you are and, therefore, what you are doing here: Destiny, Personal Power, Relationships, Forgiveness and Manifestation. As you explore these areas, you will realize your gifts and utilize them in the daily living of your life, thereby living your purpose. Personal truths will be discovered and your choices will become empowered and aligned with your highest good. More of your worth will be claimed, and your relationships will be healthier and more genuine. You will understand the power of forgiveness, and know the gifts of compassion. You will learn what matters to you.

This exploration can be compared to playing the piano. Learning to play the instrument is the journey and the music is the life you craft. As you begin you learn a few keys of the piano. Then you learn chords which you discover actually make what sounds like beautiful music. Pretty soon you're learning more and more keys and chords and you are playing elaborate compositions. Your passion and creativity are flowing, your heart is light and you are enjoying the rhythm of the music every time you play.

Power is the ability to take action. The power of choice is a foundation of this journey because you always have the ability to make a choice. We make numerous choices daily. As you understand who you are, your choices will be more aligned with your gifts, truths, reflecting your worth, rooted in compassion and reflective of what matters to you. Your choices will reflect more of who you truly are.

The path to self-discovery is as unique as you are. You decide how you want to do it, what will inspire you, what books to read, what lectures to attend, what tools to use and the beliefs you embrace. What will you do on your journey?

This is all about you, who you are and who you are becoming, what choices you will make and what changes you will seek. It can be one of the most exciting adventures of your life! As you venture along this journey, your work will be more aligned with your gifts, your choices will reflect your beliefs, you will see your worth more and more, your relationships will be rewarding, your compassion will deepen and you will know what matters to you.

Yes, life is about choices. It is also about having fun. So have fun with this journey for it is lifelong. You may get overwhelmed and frustrated at times. When you find yourself feeling any negativity at all, laugh. Laughter shifts everything immediately.

When you are in fear you are not in your power. If you feel fearful at any time, simply remember who you are. Remember who you truly are in that moment and your fear disappears. There is nothing you can't do when you know who you are.

Are you ready to know who you are and what you are doing here? Are you ready to understand the wonderful layers and depths, the magnificent Light and Love that you are?

Let's begin our explorations . . . .

Exploring Your Potential...

Chapter 2

Destiny

"It is not in the stars to hold our destiny, but in ourselves."

William Shakespeare

D estiny is all of your gifts and it's your purpose too. Your gifts are the tangible and intangible talents, qualities and abilities you naturally possess. As you utilize your gifts in daily living, you are aligning with your purpose and your destiny.

When we think of destiny we often equate it to some predetermined outcome. Destiny determines our careers, our mates and/or marital status, where we live and how we live. We wait for a sign to give us some kind of clue to our destiny. Sometimes we wait so long for the signs that we never move forward in life. We sit, waiting, afraid to make a decision, to choose a direction, to live our lives. Next thing you know, life has passed you by and you're still waiting for your destiny to be revealed.

The question of one's destiny often results in frustration. We go through life searching for purpose and meaning to our existence. This frustration waxes and wanes with life's events. Are you surprised to know that the answer to the question of destiny is within you?

What do you like to do? What skills and talents to you possess? What are your natural and creative abilities? What do you do that makes people feel good? How often do you utilize these qualities? Herein lies the answer to your question about your destiny. It is not in the stars. It is within you.

Destiny is about discovering your gifts and living your purpose. As you discover your gifts and utilize them in the daily living of your life, you are living your purpose. Expressing your gifts and sharing them with the world around you—that is why you have those gifts. Those gifts express an aspect of what you are doing here. Destiny isn't about what you "should" do. It is about living and being who you truly are.

Using your gifts brings purpose, meaning and fulfillment to your day and to your life. Here's how: Think of something you do that you love and/or that you really do well. It could be a task at work or at home, a creative hobby or a sport, for example. Imagine yourself doing that action right now and get into the feeling place of the experience. Feels pretty good, doesn't it? What do you feel? Do you feel light, free, a sense of happiness, fulfillment, maybe even joy? That is some of the feeling you get when you use one of your gifts. Now imagine having those feelings throughout your day, every day.

Here comes the fun part: revealing your gifts. The first step is to recognize some of your gifts. You may already be aware of some of your gifts. You are aware of the fact that you have a strong intuition, you're a good athlete or good with details. This process will help you become aware of more abilities that you may not recognize. Gifts are the tangible and intangible skills, talents and abilities you possess. Tangible gifts are your particular skills such as being a proficient electrician, a good mathematician, an excellent cook or a person with fine organizational skills. Intangible gifts are the "feel good" traits. These are your innate qualities that invoke emotion such as genuine kindness, a sense of humor or a warm smile.

Next you become aware of how you currently utilize those gifts at work, at home, during recreation, with friends and even with strangers. You will realize the impact they have on your day, your living and those around you. Then you will discover more ways to use these gifts and have even more purpose to your life.

To discover your gifts there are a few areas to explore. As we go through these areas one by one you will begin to recognize your gifts and may even realize a few new ones. In these explorations you will make lists in different categories. These lists can be as short or as long as you like.

First make a list of what you enjoy doing. Sometimes we like certain activities because we have a natural talent that inspires us. Do you like to draw? Is playing around in your garden, arranging flowerbeds or planting vegetables enjoyable? Do you like to throw great dinner parties?

Next list some activities you perform at work and/or at home. For example, at work you may do data entry. In your sales job you call on customers and follow up with service. A teacher creates and executes lesson plans. A parent manages many things including family finances, children's schedules and household chores.

Now make a list of what people say to you about you. "You're so funny!" "You have a great smile." "You're a terrific cook!" "How do you manage all of this so well?"

Now you have three lists that contain clues to your gifts. For example, if you like to draw, you may have a natural artistic ability. If you enjoy playing around in your garden, you could have a green thumb. Perhaps arranging dinner parties is very easy for you. You could be very organized or have a sixth sense of what people enjoy.

Data entry often requires that you are a fast and accurate typist. A sales job needs people who are good at building relationships and who are self-motivated. A parent is often good with budgeting, is efficient with time management and compassionately tends to the needs of family members. One who teaches young children is often patient, kind and creative.

Someone who is funny has a sense of humor. The source of a nice smile can be warmth. Being a great cook could mean you are creative and nurturing. The ability to manage chaos is a sign of good organizational skills.

Create one list of your gifts from the information on the previous three lists. These are some of your gifts. How is that for cool?

Now think about how you use your gifts in daily life. How are your gifts used at work, at home, during recreation, while interacting with people? Your typing skills allow you to complete your data entry duties quickly and proficiently and allow others relying on the data to do their jobs more efficiently as well. Self-motivation and the ability to build relationships help you sell your product, generate income and provide for yourself and others. Creating and patiently executing lesson plans so you may educate elementary school children in interesting ways really provides a vital service to humankind.

A person who is good at entertaining in his or her home provides an outlet for recreation, laughter and cultivating relationships. A garden created by one with a green thumb creates a beautiful space to enjoy nature and makes the world a prettier place for all!

You'll know you are using your gifts by the way you feel during the activity. Feelings invoked while using your gifts include being invigorated, motivated, peaceful, inspired, happy—to name a few.

Develop an awareness of how you use your gifts in all areas of your life. Think of ways you can use them more. What impact do you have on others while using your gifts? Warm smiles lift spirits. Good food prepared with care nourishes body and soul. Organization brings order from chaos.

The purpose of this process is to get you in touch with your gifts so you can use them more. As you do, you feel more fulfilled in your work, home and life in general. Your work has more meaning when you realize that you are using your gifts. Home life and relationships are more fulfilled when you see how your gifts impact those around you. Interaction with strangers takes on new meaning when you touch them with your gifts such as a warm smile.

Sue has a very successful career in sales. She is organized, self-motivated, hard-working—a real go-getter. Obviously these qualities help her do her job well. However, she is also very honest, trustworthy, compassionate and has a very strong Light within her. Those qualities touch everyone she encounters in her job. She can bring smiles to her clients and brighten the day just by being herself. When she has tough days at work, she remembers these qualities within her and the impact she has, and her day gets better.

After you go through this process you may want to make changes. You may interact with people more, talk to strangers while in line, take up a hobby or maybe even get a new job that really utilizes your natural talents and abilities. If you aren't in a position to change jobs easily, pay attention to how you can use your gifts more in your current professional responsibilities and interactions with others.

John is a recruiter. He is very good at his job, yet frustrated, bored and he feels his job has little meaning. As he searches for what he wants to do next, he remembers that what he does now has great meaning to those whom he helps. He finds the perfect job for others, utilizing their strengths, talents and abilities. He helps others use their gifts in their work. What a gift he is to others! That gives him more fulfillment and meaning to his day and it allows him to serve his purpose in this way.

Gayle is a mother and a homemaker and she uses her many gifts daily. In addition to managing her household, she volunteers her time to many worthy causes. She raises funds for charities, coordinates a summer camp for her church and has numerous board positions. Her gifts of natural leadership skills, organization and generosity are expressed in everything she does. A fierce and loyal friend, she is always there when needed at a moment's notice. Her sense of humor brings laughter to many situations. Gayle feels her life has meaning and purpose as she utilizes her gifts in all areas of her life.

As you can see, your gifts are not limited to your vocation. They can be utilized in all that you do, anytime you choose. A small kindness to a stranger makes you both feel good. Using your empathy to tune into a friend's needs is very helpful during troubled times. Making someone laugh is priceless. You can express your gifts anytime, anywhere and have that feeling of purpose as often as you like.

The journey of discovering your gifts is ongoing. There is no limit to the number of gifts you possess. Believe me,

16

you have many. So, what are your gifts? How do you use them? Are you living your purpose?

EXPLORATIONS

List what you enjoy doing.

List activities or duties you perform at work and/or at home.

List comments about you that people have made to you.

Take the information from the above lists and create a list of your gifts.

Think about how you currently use your gifts in your life: at work, home, with friends and family, during recreation and with strangers.

Think of more ways you can use your gifts every day.

Keep a log of how you feel as you use your gifts more and more. Note the impact you have on others.

NOTES

Exploring Your Potential...

Chapter 3

Personal Power

"True insight comes from within."

Socrates

T ruth and Choice are the roots of personal power. Truths are the beliefs that resonate within your heart. Choices are motivated by your truths. As you discover your truths, your choices become more aligned with who you truly are.

Since truths are the attitudes, ideas and values that resonate within your heart, it's not about what you "should" believe or what is a right or a wrong way of thinking. There is no dogma in truth. It's about what feels right to you.

When your actions are motivated by your clear truths, your choice at any moment will be apparent. In a specific

21

situation, if you don't like what you are experiencing with the result or the outcome, check the truth that motivated the choice and see where you can make a change and therefore make a different choice. Personal power is identifying your truths and making choices that reflect who you REALLY are, choices that are based on your clear truths.

As children we are taught certain beliefs and values by our parents, teachers, society and religious institutions. We take these teachings as truths. They establish the foundation for our beliefs and our value systems. As we get older we begin to think for ourselves. We question things, become thoughtful on how we really feel about the beliefs that created our foundation as well as other information that crosses our paths.

Your heart holds the answer to the question, "What is truth?" Love is at the core of your heart and love is never wrong. To know if something is your truth, tune in and feel it in your heart center. When you hear a belief, does your heart feel light and free or does it feel heavy and tight? If your heart center feels light and free, that is your truth. If it feels heavy and tight, that is a belief that does not resonate with you.

Read the following list and see what your heart feels. Which statements reflect your truth? Which ones do not? Some of these are more universal truths while others are more subjective. Some are obvious and others may take some thought. Remember, there is no right or wrong answer. Your answers will be as unique as you are.

Murder is wrong.

Stealing is okay.

Life is hard.

Puppies are cute.

The sky is blue.

God exists.

Your marital/relationship status determines your worth as a woman.

Your financial status determines your worth as a man.

Chocolate is the best food in the world.

Now that you have an understanding of the way a truth feels compared to a belief that is false, let's discover some of your truths.

Make a list of a few things that you believe. Include categories such as religion and spirituality, death and the afterlife, career, happiness, gender roles, money and personal responsibility. Do you believe money is evil? Do you believe in reincarnation or that we have one lifetime? What are your ideas about gender roles and the place for women and men in marriage, workplace or politics? Do you feel you need a mate to validate your existence and worth as a person? Write down the first things that pop into your head.

Read each one and verify that it is or is not really your truth. How does your heart center feel when you read it? For example, say you wrote that you believe we have one lifetime. As you read that you feel a slight discomfort in your chest. Why? Do you really believe that we only have one lifetime? Was that a belief you came to on your own or is it something you were taught by your family, religion

24

or society? Go within and get clear on how you really feel about the truth. Perhaps the idea that we have many lifetimes feels better to you. If so, then that may be your truth. If you feel light in your chest when reading that statement, it validates what you believe to be true.

Other people's truths can influence our own. They can introduce us to new ideas and expand our horizons. We can discover our own truths this way.

Discovering your truths is key to understanding your personal power. Your choices are motivated by your truths and reflect who you are. You make a choice that produces an outcome. Your life becomes a reflection of your beliefs and conviction. Personal power allows us to make such choices, to review outcomes and to choose again if necessary.

If you don't like a situation in your life, go to the truth that motivated the choice. What does it say? Is it really how you feel? Your reality holds the answer. Go to the truth, change it to reflect who you are and what you really believe, and make a new choice. Now that is power!

Dan had been in his job for six years. He worked very long hours, had very little free time, yet generated a large income. His life revolved around work.

In the beginning he enjoyed his job but over time he became increasingly unhappy. He decided to explore the idea of making a change. Making money is what brought him happiness which is why he chose to take this job. It had brought him fulfillment for many years but that was no longer happening.

The truth that motivated his choice to take this job was that money was one of the most important things in his life. He still enjoyed making money; however, a balanced life became more essential. Dan changed jobs and chose a career that allowed him to make money and work less hours so he could have more free time. Although he took a slight cut in pay, he joined a health club, made new friends, discovered new hobbies and even pursued philanthropic ventures. His life had a renewed sense of fulfillment and happiness.

Truths can change and evolve as we do. Your truth is your truth in the moment you make a choice. If you don't like the outcome of the choice, go to the heart of the truth and see if it reflects who you truly are. In Dan's case his life lacked balance and that eventually became significant to his well-being.

To see how this works in your life, think of a choice you made that had desirable results. Now recognize the truth behind that choice.

Say you recently moved to a new city. You feel very happy there and you have made new friends quickly, gotten involved in the community and have spent lots of time outdoors year-round because of the mild climate. Next we'll explore the motive behind your choice.

Prior to moving you lived in your hometown all your life. Many generations lived in this town and few moved away.

The norm was to stay near your roots and near family. Your family believed this strongly and they were very vocal about it as you announced your decision to relocate. You wanted to try something new and different. You believed that it was okay to leave your hometown and begin a new life. It wasn't that you didn't love your family or your hometown. Spreading your wings and finding your own way was important to you so you chose this new experience. That choice was based on a truth that reflected who you truly are.

Secondly, think of a choice you made that had an undesirable result. Your current profession makes you unhappy, yet you chose it due to family pressures and expectations when your dreams were different. In this case your truth at the time was that following your family's wishes was more important than following your own. Explore whether or not that is a reflection of who you truly are. You may realize that following your dreams is now more important than making other people happy.

The beauty of all of this is the power of choice. If you don't like a situation, change it by making a different choice. Discovering your truth that is at the root of the choice you made can help you know what is right for you.

We may not always like the choices we have made but we always have a choice. Isn't it grand?

Mistakes are choices that produce undesired outcomes. If you feel you made a mistake, choose again! This frees you from guilt and blame for the mistake. You don't have to be held hostage by your mistake. Realize your personal power and make a new choice!

For example, your friend, Marla, told you something in confidence and you shared it with Judy. Judy told Marla and now you're in hot water. Marla is very upset, hurt and feels betrayed. She's not sure if she wants to continue the friendship. You feel guilty and ashamed for the consequences of your choice. One choice is to apologize and create a different result, one of healing and remorse. You may still feel remorseful but you can release yourself from the guilt and shame because you took action to make amends. Marla may or may not decide to maintain the friendship but your new choice allows you to move forward.

Standing in your personal power takes the courage to make choices that reflect who you truly are. This can create resistance and fears such as, *What will people think if I believe this? What will my family think? Friends, co-workers, society? How will this change my life? What will happen to my current relationships?*

As you reveal your own truths and understand your personal power, yes, things can change. Some relationships may need to be redefined and others released altogether. Past choices may be replaced with new decisions. Change is always good. Always. Your choices and, therefore, your reality will reflect more of who you truly are as you reveal it and with that comes more happiness, fulfillment and peace.

So, what are your truths? Which decisions that you have made reflect who you truly are? Which ones do not? Discover your truths and the nature of choice and you will understand your personal power. That is who you truly are.

EXPLORATIONS

Make a list of what you believe. Include categories such as religion/spirituality, death, career/job, self-esteem, happiness, gender roles, personal responsibility and money.

Go through each one and take a few moments to feel it. How does the truth feel to you. Does your heart feel light and free or heavy and tight?

List a choice you've made in the past with a desirable outcome. What beliefs motivated this choice?

List a choice you made in the past with an undesirable outcome. What beliefs motivated this choice? Examine those beliefs more carefully. How do those truths feel to you? Do they feel heavy and tight? Explore variations of those truths and continue on until your new truth feels light and free.

Now make a new list of your truths that are feeling light and free in your heart.

List some different choices you can make that reflect these truths.

Create awareness within you of discovering your truth. Become thoughtful of what you hear on television or in conversation, what you read, what you see around you and consider how it feels to you. Take what feels right into your heart and disregard the rest. Find out YOUR truths and make choices that reflect who you truly are.

NOTES

Chapter 4

Relationships

"Self-love, my liege, is not so vile a sin as self-neglecting."

William Shakespeare

Relationships are a reflection of how much worth you recognize in yourself. We all have one hundred percent worth. We don't have to earn it, we cannot lose it and it cannot be taken away. By looking at your relationships you can see how much worth you have claimed and how much is still waiting to be claimed.

Your worth is the whole of who you are and all that you are. It is your light, love, compassion, generosity, quirkiness, oddities and idiosyncrasies. Claiming your worth is knowing that you are valuable, lovable, and you deserve to be loved and valued. It is knowing that you are whole and complete just as you are. All that you need is within you because you have worth.

As you claim more of your worth, your life changes around you. Others will reflect your worth back to you more because you are able to see it more. All of your relationships will improve—the new ones you attract and those you currently have in your life. Your relationships will be healthier and more fulfilling.

How we feel about ourselves determines what we seek in relationships, how we allow ourselves to be treated and how we treat others. This applies to all relationships—those with significant others, friends, family, co-workers, even strangers. The worth we feel is mirrored in our relationships. For example, if you don't respect yourself, you will allow yourself to be treated with disrespect. If you are insecure, you may put others down just so you will feel better.

Relationships offer opportunities to identify how much worth we recognize and how much we don't. If you know you are lovable and valuable, you only accept behavior that reflects that. If you don't know this, you are more inclined to allow behavior which does not reflect this. It's about knowing that you are lovable and valuable always. Not sometimes, but always.

If you think you don't have value, you will choose a partner who doesn't think you do either. If you realize the value you really have, your partner will too. The more you know how lovable and valuable you truly are, the more everyone around you will see that. No one can see it if you don't!

We look externally to provide us with what we can only give ourselves. What we are often seeking is validation that we are lovable. Already we are all one hundred percent worthy, valuable and lovable. If we look to others to validate this or to give us this, it is because we don't see that we already have it. We don't trust that we are the only ones who can give this to us.

If we do not see our worth, our choices tend to be motivated by a fear of losing love and out of a fear that we are not lovable. This fear is reflected back to us everywhere—through family, friends, even strangers. We take others' actions towards us to mean we are not lovable. If you know who you truly are, you will understand that this is a lie. Then your relationships are more centered on the experience and the expression of love and you are not trying to prove that you are lovable.

You fear, for example, that your girlfriend may leave you so you spend a great deal of energy trying to prevent that from happening. You make yourself available for her all of the time, compromising your preferences and needs to accommodate hers. If your girlfriend leaves, you think you are not lovable. Your relationship is focused on the potential for being abandoned instead of experiencing what the relationship may have to offer. Even if your girlfriend leaves, she's not abandoning you. No one can abandon you but you. In this scenario you have abandoned yourself by not knowing that you are lovable and valuable and by putting all of your worth in the existence of that relationship.

We spend so much energy on relationships with others. Imagine what would happen if we took even a small amount of that energy and focused it on the relationship with ourselves!

We all have needs and preferences. Basic needs include food, shelter, clothing, et cetera. Preferences could include gourmet food, a house with a big yard and extra bedrooms, the ability to afford luxuries and designer clothing. The needs are for survival. Preferences are the extras we want in life as pleasures.

Regarding relationships, choices made from the place of need versus preference yield very different results. To "need" a relationship suggests that it is something you lack and that you require for survival. You feel you are inadequate, incomplete, and insufficient and, therefore, need a relationship to give you that which you lack.

When you come from a place of preference, you recognize your wholeness and completeness. You desire a relationship as an experience to enrich and enhance your life in different ways. You already provide everything that you need for yourself. Relationships are experiences to express and delight in love in different and unique ways.

The more you provide what you need for yourself, the more you'll get what you want in your relationships. The focus of your relationships will be more about love and less about getting what you need because you lack something.

To see how much worth you have recognized, start by understanding your relationship with yourself. You are the only one who can give you what you need, so look at what you want in a relationship and see how much you are giving to yourself. This way you can have more genuine relationships rooted in love and you will not be looking to others to give you what you need.

Start this process by becoming aware of your self-talk. Spend the next week or so paying attention to what you say to yourself. You may be surprised how hard you are on yourself. Do you say things like "I'm so stupid"? "How could I have done that?" "I'm so fat, ugly, my nose is too big. . . ." Are you constantly apologizing to others for behavior or mistakes? Do you belittle yourself to others? Keep a journal of these comments and experiences. This will illuminate how you feel about yourself.

Next make a list of the qualities you want in a relationship. Choose just a few to start. For example, let's say you want love, respect, caring, sharing and companionship. Go down the list and see how much of all of these qualities you offer yourself. If you want these qualities, you have to give them to yourself first.

How much do you love yourself? Are you constantly criticizing yourself? Are you patient and gentle with yourself or are you always beating yourself up over what you do, say, how you look, et cetera? Refer to your list of self-talk for more insight.

Do you respect yourself? How do you allow people to treat you? If you allow people to take advantage of you, chances are you don't respect yourself as much as you could. Do you allow people to belittle or criticize you often?

Caring is vital to a relationship. Do you care for yourself? What do you do for your health and well-being? Do you eat well? Exercise? Do you do things you enjoy or is it always about everyone else's needs?

How much of yourself do you share with others? Are you very guarded and generally you don't let people see the real you for fear they may not like you?

How good of a companion are you to yourself? Do you do things alone or only when you have a friend to accompany you? Do you enjoy your own company? Are you comfortable spending time alone? If you don't like being alone with yourself, why would anyone else want to be with you?

Begin to give yourself more love, respect, caring, sharing and companionship and you will bring more of those qualities into your relationships.

Let's examine some of your current or past relationships. One indicator of your claimed worth is how you feel in certain relationships. This will vary with each relationship and at different times in the relationship.

Think of someone you know with whom you feel at ease, cherished, safe and loved. It could be a friend, relative or significant other. When you are with this person, you are confident, relaxed, secure and comfortable being yourself the majority of the time. Think about specific qualities you feel such as attractive, interesting and intelligent. You are attractive, interesting and intelligent already. The relationship is not giving you those qualities. It is reflecting qualities back to you which you know to be true.

Any relationship reflects how much you know that you are lovable and how valuable you are. It doesn't reflect that you ARE lovable and valuable as if outside forces are giving you these qualities. It reflects how aware YOU are of those facts. The relationship is reflecting the worth you have claimed because you are comfortable seeing it in this relationship.

Next think of a relationship where you feel stressed, anxious and edgy, not completely comfortable being yourself the majority of the time. This is possibly a situation where you don't know that you are lovable and valuable.

Focus on how you feel around this person and how you act around him or her. If you feel "less than" around your friends or co-workers because they are better looking, smarter, funnier, you aren't recognizing your own beauty, intelligence or sense of humor. If you are constantly criticizing how others look, dress or act, it shows you aren't comfortable with yourself. If you're thinking someone is smarter than you are and that makes you not very smart, this is your opportunity to discover your hidden worth. If you think someone is better looking and therefore you are unattractive, it is another opportunity to open your mind to your hidden worth. If you think someone is so confident because they are so fabulous and you are so self-conscious and, therefore, a loser, here is another great opportunity to see your hidden worth. Remember, it's only hidden from you. It's a wonderful time to see more of who you truly are. What you see in others that you feel you lack are qualities you just don't recognize in yourself.

No matter what is going on externally, you are whole and complete because you have worth. All you need to do is own it. As you own it little by little, piece by piece, moment by moment you will experience that wholeness that you are. You will know more of who you truly are—someone who is lovable and valuable.

Here are some examples of relationship reflections when your worth is hidden from your view: If you are attracted to partners who are emotionally unavailable, perhaps you don't see that you are worthy of being loved. If a friend uses you, takes advantage of you, constantly belittles and criticizes you, your value is hidden from your view. Being uncomfortable with compliments could indicate that you're hiding from seeing that particular attribute in yourself.

Another example relates to feeling as though you always have to "do" all the time in order to receive love. It's as if you have to earn it in some way. You are not seeing your true worth. To love means to give and receive love, not just give it. If you are uncomfortable receiving love, you are uncomfortable seeing your worth.

If you're critical of others, it is because you are critical of yourself. Being patient and compassionate with others is because you are patient and kind with yourself. When you find yourself saying negative things to others, pay attention to what you are saying to yourself!

Again, you are the only one who can give you what you need. The more you give to yourself, the more you will get out of your relationships. If your mother's approval is something you need, you'll spend lots of energy trying to gain her approval. You may never get it but you will always try. If you approve of yourself, the need to seek it from your mother or anyone else disappears. Then your relationship with your mother can be more real and be more about the love you have for each other and less about gaining approval. Once you approve of yourself you will not need to seek the approval of others.

Let's look at Liz and Eric. Liz was involved with Eric for about a year. They had a unique connection, a good deal in common and lots of fun together. Eric came and went as he pleased, called Liz when he felt like it and saw her only when it suited him. He wasn't accommodating to her invitations or requests. This made Liz very insecure and self-conscious. She never knew when she'd see him or even if she'd see him again. However, she really liked Eric and didn't want him to leave so she tolerated his behavior. She was nervous, anxious and self-conscious around him all the time. She began to put his needs before hers, always accommodating him in hopes that he would need her and, therefore, not leave the relationship.

As time passed Liz realized that this was not a good situation for her. It was causing her pain and much stress. She realized that a part of her felt she deserved to be treated with disregard and disrespect because she was allowing Eric to treat her this way. Liz discovered more of her worth that had continued to remain hidden because of this relationship. She was in fact lovable and valuable and no longer wanted this treatment. She ended the relationship and her next partner treated her kindly and respectfully because she did not tolerate anything less.

Pets are excellent mirrors of your worth. A dog, for example, loves you unconditionally, no matter what. All you have to do is provide the basic needs for your pooch—food, water, health maintenance—and he will love you always. You don't have to earn your dog's love. Even if you're gone ten hours a day or travel five days a week, your pup will still love you. Pets also teach us to receive love without having to "earn" it. If you have a pet, tune in to how your pet makes you feel. This is an excellent way to see how much worth you have claimed.

So, what are your relationships showing you? What is your relationship with yourself and how is that reflected in your relationships with others? Develop a strong relationship with yourself and know that you are lovable and valuable always and all of your relationships will be genuine.

EXPLORATIONS

Part 1:

Create an awareness of how you see yourself.

Describe how you see yourself. Note your self-talk.

List how you think others see you. List comments others have made to you.

Compare how you see yourself to the ways you feel others see you.

Part 2:

List the qualities you want in a relationship.

Note how many of these qualities you are giving to yourself. List ways you could improve.

Part 3:

Distinguish the differences between relationships that reflect the worth you have claimed and relationships that show where your worth is hidden from your view.

Think about a relationship in your life. He or she could be a friend, a spouse, a co-worker or family member. Think of someone with whom you feel relaxed, light and comfortable.

List specifically how being around this person makes you feel: beautiful, smart, capable, interesting, funny, lovable, et cetera. See your worth reflected back to you in this situation illuminated by these emotions. Embrace these qualities for you already possess them.

Now think about another relationship where you feel stressed, anxious, uptight, nervous and self-conscious. Pay attention to your self-talk when you are with that person or after you have been with him or her.

List what you think that person is showing you about yourself. For example, do you feel he or she is smarter than you are and therefore you aren't very smart?

Remember, you already HAVE worth. This process is to help you recognize it and then claim your true worth as yours.

Part 4:

Recognize how your beliefs and attitudes of yourself are motivating your choices in your current relationships.

What changes could you make in your relationship with yourself?

What changes could you make in your relationships with others?

Create an awareness of how much you know you are lovable and valuable. In doing so you can embrace the areas where it is visible and explore the areas where it is not so visible.

NOTES

Chapter 5

Forgiveness

"The weak can never forgive.
Forgiveness is the attribute of the strong."

Mahatma Gandhi

Forgiveness connects you with who you truly are as it deepens your compassion for yourself and others. It allows you to discover the gift in every situation. As a result, you will be free of the past so that you can create a future with less stress, guilt and shame.

When we are mistreated in some way, we can feel emotions such as pain, anger, hurt, resentment, shame and blame, to name a few. These are all very real emotions that result from our experiences. Some choose to cling to these emotions and to the past. "Forgiveness is weak!" they say.

"How can I ever forgive her for what she did?" "If I forgive him, that means I'm condoning his behavior."

Hanging onto these feelings prevents us from experiencing who we truly are. Abundant love, happiness, peace and joy are all ours for the taking if we are willing to receive. As you release the energy of the past, you are free to receive more of life's gifts and you know more of who you are.

How do you know if forgiveness is needed? If you are feeling the kinds of emotions listed above, chances are there is some forgiveness work to be done. When doing forgiveness work, you are forgiving the WHY someone did whatever he or she did, not necessarily WHAT they did. In this process you are in search of understanding the WHY.

Every action is motivated by an emotion. Discovering the WHY helps you gain understanding of the emotions behind the actions and this leads you to compassion. As you deepen your compassion you become more of who you truly are. It isn't about placing blame on yourself or another. It is about understanding so you can deepen your compassion.

Another gem in forgiveness is that it allows you to find the gift in every situation. Every experience contains a gift, no matter how unpleasant the experience may be. Finding the gift in each situation helps you to release the past, find purpose and meaning in life's events and that brings you a sense of peace.

Forgiveness may seem like a daunting endeavor. You may wonder where to begin. Start with forgiving yourself. You can't forgive anyone else until you have forgiven yourself. "Forgive myself for what? I was the one who was mistreated." Forgive yourself for allowing the situation. It is not necessary to blame yourself but to acknowledge that you somehow allowed it into your reality.

For example, you could be walking through a parking lot to your car after work and someone jumps you, punches you out and steals your wallet. You didn't ask them to do this nor did you want them to. But it happened. You may blame yourself for being in that place at that time, walking to your car alone or parking in a dark corner. You may be furious at yourself for not fighting back, even though the perpetrator had a knife. Many thoughts may go through your mind. Whether these points are valid or not, they are valid to you in this moment and that is why you need to forgive yourself. In your perception you are angry and upset for putting yourself in a situation where you would be the victim of a crime. This crime could have happened in broad daylight in the middle of a crowd of people in the safest part of town and you'd still be mad at yourself. That's what we often do. We are very critical of ourselves.

So this is where you start. Forgive yourself for what you think you did to allow the situation. This is very subjective. Someone in the same situation may think they did different things to allow the event. The details don't matter. It's the emotions behind the details that you need to release.

Think about the event, what you experienced and how you felt. Process the experience in your mind and heart.

Understand why you did what you did. Perhaps you had to park there because you were late to work. Your friend who always walks with you to the parking lot wasn't available that day. Perhaps go a little deeper. Do you have an attitude that "bad things always happen to me" or "people are always out to get me"? Take responsibility here and see what's really going on. Understand your emotions behind your behavior and connect with your compassion for yourself. This can relate to seeing your true worth.

Next find the gift in this experience. There is a gift in every situation. Discovering the gifts also helps you shift your perception. You really didn't like that job anymore and this motivated you to make a change. You've always felt like a victim in life and now you don't want to, so you work to end that pattern. Maybe you hit it off with the police officer at the scene and you're dating now. Who knows? The point is there is a gift for you to find. You can do it.

Then forgive yourself. Release your anger, blame, guilt and shame towards yourself. See yourself in your mind's eye and forgive yourself. Embrace yourself and surround yourself with Light or whatever feels natural to you. Feel the heaviness lift out of your heart. You may need to do this process a few times or once may be all that you need.

Now it's time to forgive the other person. You can't always forgive someone for WHAT they did so you're going to forgive WHY they did it. Remember, every action is motivated by an emotion. In this phase, you gain an understanding of the emotions behind why they did what they did. You don't need to talk to this person to understand this. Simply open your heart to your compassion. This is also why it helps to forgive yourself first. If you aren't able to have compassion for yourself, you can't have it for others.

Think of the event once again. Focus on the behavior of the person. Tune in to the possible emotions motivating his or her actions. If you truly have no idea, just list something. If you've forgiven yourself and your heart is more open, it's easier to understand. Some possible explanations could be that this person was on drugs and therefore was in great emotional pain because of having this addiction. Or this person may have been raised in a home where violence and crime are common and acceptable behavior. Maybe he blames everyone else for his misfortune and consequently took it out on you. There are many possibilities here. You are not condoning, excusing or approving the behavior but you are gaining an understanding so you can forgive and release this from your life.

Once you have this understanding, forgive that person and release the whole situation. Open to your compassion, see that person in your mind's eye and forgive him or her. Within your mind, embrace that person, surround him or her in Light or do whatever feels natural to you.

Now discover the gift in the situation. You know there is one. Perhaps this is why you allowed this into your reality—so that you could receive this gift. Receive the gift and find the purpose to the experience.

Let's return to Liz and Eric. To recap, Eric treated Liz with disregard and disrespect and showed little concern for her feelings. Once Liz decided to end the relationship, she had to forgive herself first for allowing that treatment. She had to go into WHY she allowed it. She examined the emotions behind her actions. She had already learned that she disregarded and disrespected herself and felt unworthy and undeserving of being loved, cherished and respected. As Liz understood this, she was able to forgive herself. This released the negativity in her and she filled that space with more compassion for herself.

Forgiving Eric wasn't so easy. It took time for Liz to understand why he treated her this way. She was so kind, understanding and compassionate to him, always making herself available to him, no matter the disruption to her day. How could he treat her this way when she was so giving? What could possibly be the explanation other than he was a selfish jerk? Through this process she realized there was a lot behind this selfish jerk.

Eric was very insecure and terrified of intimacy. He grew up in an abusive home and never learned how to connect with people on an intimate level. He was detached and disconnected from everyone, including himself. It's what he learned as a child and he never realized his own patterns. Once Liz grasped this, she developed compassion for him and was able to forgive Eric for WHY he treated her this way. She didn't want to resume the relationship or save him as she might have done before.

The gift in this situation was realizing that she deserved to be treated with respect. In her quest for forgiveness Liz discovered more of her own true worth. The negativity and regret were released, her heart lightened and she was able to fill it with more love, thereby attracting more love into her life.

You don't have to have a conversation with the person for this process. In some instances, the person may be deceased or may be a stranger, or you just don't want to talk to that person. This isn't about that person. It's about you. He or she doesn't need to know you've forgiven him or her. That person will have a knowing on some level. The one who needs to know is you. Take as much time as you need without swimming in it too long. You may need to repeat this a few times, so you truly forgive, or once may do it.

This process applies to everything, big or small. Say someone cuts you off in traffic. You get very angry about it. It may be momentary anger but you really feel it. Why hang onto it? In order to shift it, think about the reasons why he or she could have done this. Maybe he or she is late, or driving to aid a sick child, or just left a doctor's appointment where he or she received some bad news. Maybe he or she is just plain aggressive and is worthy of compassion for the pain felt that causes such aggression. You never know what's going on with someone else but if you want to shift your energy, find the potential emotions for the WHY of the behavior and you will find compassion. That shifts everything.

The more understanding we have, the less we reach for blame. We deepen our compassion for ourselves and others, find purpose in life's events and free ourselves from the past. What follows is a life with more love, caring and less pain, guilt and regret.

EXPLORATIONS

Think of a situation that needs forgiveness.

Write down what happened and how it made you feel.

Go through the process of forgiving yourself. Understand why you think you allowed this. Find out what the gift is from this experience.

Forgive yourself. Open to compassion and release yourself from the binding emotions.

Repeat this process as needed.

Next, forgive the other person. Think about the event again.

Go through the understanding step.

Open your heart and understand why that person did what he or she did. If you need to, see that person in your mind and tune in to him or her. Trust that you're getting what you need.

Once you have the understanding, forgive that person. Repeat as needed.

Find the gift in the experience.

Now you're open to receive more of the gifts life has to offer. Note how your life begins to change.

NOTES

Chapter 6

Manifestation

"The quality, not the longevity of one's life, is what is important."

Martin Luther King, Jr.

The power to create what you want in life is yours. You have the ability to change who you are. You can change your life. This process reveals the fears and negativities that need to be released in order to progress. Be ready to create miracles and show the world who you are and what you will do!

You may have heard about the law of attraction. You attract in your life what you focus your attention upon. What you think you create. Say affirmations, keep your thoughts positive and what you desire will manifest. It's that easy. But it's not necessarily that simple!

Chances are you've experienced the law of attraction but you don't realize it. You may have thought of someone and then they called you or you ran into them somewhere. On a trip to the mall you zero in on finding a parking space in front and it's there when you arrive. You make a comment that you are hungry. Moments later there is a knock on your door and a gift box of cookies is delivered to you. These are examples of the law of attraction. What we think, we create. It's happening anyway so you may as well channel it to manifest what you want!

So, what do you want? Manifestation isn't just about material things. If you want money, clothes, homes, cars, you can have it. The gifts of manifestation are not just getting what you want. Manifestation offers the opportunity to know more of who you are because you can learn what matters to you. This engages your heart in the process of manifestation and, as we know, that is where your truth lies.

Many of us want things such as fulfilling employment, rewarding relationships, comfortable financial means and good health. But why do you want those things? Why does fulfilling work matter to you? Perhaps so that you can feel fulfilled using your skills and talents. You may want rewarding relationships to enrich and enhance your life, to share experiences and life's journey or to create a family. Comfortable financial means may matter to you so that you can provide for your family or give yourself a few of life's luxuries. Good health is key for you to be able to feel good and to enjoy a quality life.

Maybe you want to be of service more. Being of service is rewarding and gratifying. It takes us outside of ourselves and opens us to compassion and caring for others. More free time may be important to you in order to spend more time with family, develop a new hobby or to volunteer for your favorite cause. When you learn what matters to you, the pleasure of receiving what you want goes to the next level. You have more appreciation, gratitude and enjoyment with the things you manifest. It is a reflection of who you are because you have engaged your heart in order to create what you want.

Manifestation is a tool to script your life exactly how you want it. So, again, what do you want and why do you want it? There are no right or wrong answers. It's important to know why you want what you want. It helps you understand more of who you are and also sends a clearer message to the universe. The universe will give you exactly what you ask.

Try it now. Think of something you want like a new, red sports car. Focus your attention to it. Think of it as if you already have the car. See yourself driving in the shiny, new, red sports car and having a great time. You can create affirmations to keep the positive thoughts flowing around this if you choose.

This technique requires more than focusing your thoughts. The real work comes in when you are aligning your feelings with your thoughts. Think of the new, red sports car again. Feel it as if you already have it. Feel what it's like to be driving the car down the road. Now pay attention to your feelings around having this shiny, new car. Do you feel excited or do you sense a pit in your chest?

Getting your thoughts and feelings in alignment is key. Your feelings will tell you where you are in your clarity of knowing what you want and why. Your feelings reveal any fear or negativity that may be hanging around. As you're feeling what you want, what's really going on in your heart? It's similar to discovering your truths. Does your heart feel light and free when you feel what it's like to have this? Or does it feel heavy and tight? If it feels heavy and tight, you have more work to do.

Go in there and understand what that fear or negativity is. There are many possibilities such as feeling you don't deserve what it is that you want. In this example maybe you feel a car like that is just too extravagant and not appropriate. In other examples perhaps it's because you're not worthy of this happiness or that love. A fear of success is common too. How will you change if you have this success you want? How will others see you or treat you? Maybe it's doubt you feel in the ability to truly manifest what you want. Perhaps you were raised to believe that life is hard so manifesting things easily isn't possible. You could feel guilty for having all of this money, love and happiness when others are struggling.

Refer to exploration sections in previous chapters if you need clarity about what is blocking you. Love of self is key to manifesting what you want. If you were raised to believe that life is hard, this could keep you from manifesting what you want. Forgive yourself for having these feelings and patterns and forgive those who taught them to you.

Melinda has worked on manifesting a relationship with a life partner. She focuses on what she wants, writes a list of appealing qualities in a man, sees the relationship in her life and gets into the feeling place of having it. She's also written affirmations to assist in the process. Frustration sets in because she hasn't manifested a life partner. Melinda realizes that her thoughts and feelings may not be in alignment. When she feels this relationship in her life she gets a pit in her chest. It doesn't feel light and free most of the time but heavy and tight.

Upon more introspection she grasped the truth that she really didn't feel worthy of being loved to this degree or that she deserved this relationship. She didn't see that she was lovable and valuable. Subsequently, she noticed that same pattern in her past relationships and it explained a great deal about her love of self. Melinda did the work to discover more of who she truly is and she released the fear and negativity. Going back to her manifesting technique, she focused on her thoughts and feelings of having this life partner. Her heart felt light and free, she knew her thoughts and feelings were in alignment and it was just a matter of time.

This process is a catalyst for becoming aware of your thoughts. When you are working to manifest something, you focus your thoughts on what you want. As you do this you become more and more aware of all of your thoughts and how positive or negative they are. You may be surprised at how many negative thoughts go through your head. It is also an opportunity to discover more of who you are through the clarity revealed when connecting with your feelings around what you want.

When doing this work focus on what you want, not who you want or how you'll get it. Focusing on the WHAT allows the universe to fill in the details of the WHO and the HOW. You could include intentions like "this or better, without harm" or "for my highest good". It keeps you detached from the outcome, yet still brings what you want. If you don't get this, something better will appear in its place or could be on its way.

If you want a job at Company XYZ and you focus all of your attention on it, you will get the job at Company XYZ. In the meantime Company ABC may have an even better job for you that is more suited to what you want but you missed it because you were so focused on Company XYZ.

When manifesting a relationship, focus on what you want, include the feelings and the qualities and let the universe bring you the person in any way the universe wants to bring him or her to you.

Michael was frustrated at work. He loved his job and was well compensated. His career choice allowed him to utilize his gifts and creativity and it fed his passions. Yet he was constantly complaining about things regarding work.

One day his wife brought this chronic complaining to his attention. She knew how fulfilling this job was for him and couldn't understand his frustration and, frankly, was tired of hearing him complain.

Michael was familiar with the idea of manifestation. He used manifestation techniques to draw this dream job into his life. Obviously he wanted something to change but was unclear about what specifically. He spent some time getting clear on what he wanted, on what mattered to him and why. He thought about his job, felt how much he enjoyed it, but there was an aching feeling in his chest. At that moment his five-year-old son walked in the room and wanted to play. Michael's heart warmed and he was elated. That's when his light bulb went off. What he wanted was more free time to be with his family!

He had no idea how he was going to make this happen. He worked about fifty hours a week, brought work home with him some evenings and had the bi-monthly two-day business trip. Once he let go of figuring out how this was going to happen and who could help him make it happen, he focused his thoughts and feelings on what he wanted. He saw and felt he wanted to spend more time with his wife and kids without compromising the quality of his work.

A few weeks later his boss came in and said that Michael was getting an assistant to help him with his workload. It was exactly what he needed! He was able to lighten his workload and better manage his time doing what needed to be done. His work week shortened to an average of forty-five hours a week and he was bringing work home less frequently.

Trust plays a big role in this. Trust yourself that you can manifest what you want. Know that as you understand more of who you are, you will manifest more of what you want. Trust the universe to bring it to you even if it isn't on your timetable. Stay detached but actively focused on your thoughts and feelings. Learn what matters to you. It will bring more enjoyment and appreciation to what you create. Have fun and enjoy what life brings you!

EXPLORATIONS

Write down something you want.

Think of why you want it, why it matters to you and write it down. Feel why it matters to you.

Get into the feeling place of having what it is that you want. Feel it as if you already have it. Note what you're feeling. Start with observing if your heart feels light and free or heavy and tight.

If your heart feels heavy and tight, do the work to discover the fear and negativity behind it. Refer to other chapter explorations if necessary. Take as long as you need here. Release the fear and negativity patterns that no longer serve you.

If your heart feels light and free, think again about what you want. Focus your thoughts and feelings on having this in your life. If you like affirmations, create some and write them down. Set your intention of "this or better, without harm to others."

Pay attention to your thoughts throughout your day. Are they negative or are they positive? Create an ongoing awareness of your thoughts and shift them to positive when needed.

Release this to the universe and trust, trust, trust that the universe will give you what you want to create.

NOTES

Exploring Your Potential...

87

Exploring Your Potential...

Chapter 7

Discover Your Teacher Within

"Nothing changes until you do."

Lazaris

Become your own teacher using life as your mirror and intuition as your guide. Your outer world is a reflection of your inner world. How we react and respond to events is a direct reflection of what is going on inside of us. Experiences are opportunities to see negativities and fears to be released and to reveal parts of yourself that you want to embrace or expand. Your responses and reactions change as you do. If want to change your situation, change yourself. "Nothing changes until you do."

You create occasions to express your gifts in order to understand and live your purpose. As you bring forth experiences to illuminate your truths, you discover what you believe in your heart. As you bring relationships into your life you learn more about yourself and claim more of your worth. If you have been producing opportunities for forgiveness, you will understand the emotions behind the actions, thereby deepening compassion. By examining what you are attracting to your life you understand what you want to release and embrace.

What is going on outside of us is a direct reflection of what is going on inside of us at that moment. Our outer reality is created by our perceptions. If you feel everyone is out to get you, you will have experiences where you feel you are the victim of a situation. If you change that belief and realize the power that you have, you will have less experiences where you feel people are out to get you. If you feel insecure and worthless, your experiences will mirror that belief. If you feel centered, self-loving and confident in who you are, life will reflect that too.

We react and respond to situations based on how we are feeling about ourselves. Let's say you encounter someone at the market who is angry and cranky. They push themselves through the aisles and cut in front of you at the check-out line. If you tend to feel like a victim and that everyone is constantly pushing you around, you may react strongly to this person's behavior and fly off the handle.

On the other hand, maybe you didn't react much at all. They really didn't bother you and you even felt a little sorry for this person because they seemed so unhappy. Chances are in that moment you felt centered, confident and self-loving. This experience showed you aspects of yourself that you want to embrace and expand upon—your love for yourself and for others plus patience and confidence. If you encounter angry people often, you may want to examine your own unacknowledged anger. These are good opportunities to see aspects in yourself that you want to release.

We all have moments when we don't feel great. You will want to assess and examine the mirrors that repeat themselves. It's not about judging where you are or how you behave. It's about examining situations to gain information and assess where you are and where you want to be.

Janet constantly felt criticized. Her family, friends, co-workers and even strangers were always criticizing her. She felt beaten down, demoralized and plain stupid. As she began to understand that life is a mirror, she realized that they were reflecting her strong sense of insecurity and that she was very critical of herself. She decided to work on her insecurities, understanding her worth, gifts, compassion and many other aspects of herself. Soon she noticed people were less critical of her. Were they really? Or was it because Janet had more confidence in who she was? Either way she changed herself so her outer world changed too.

Life is about choices. There is no "supposed to" and there are no "should haves" or "could haves"—only choice. You are where you are supposed to be in this moment because you choose to be there. Remember, power is the ability to choose. The power is yours to change it or embrace it. It always has been. Choice is a gift, so claim it and create the life you want.

Use life to show you where you are and decide where you want to be in each moment. The mirrors are everywhere. Pay attention to what the mirrors are showing you and what your intuition is telling you. If something doesn't feel right, explore an alternative that does. If you don't like what you see in any given moment, change it. Make a different choice. If you like what you see, embrace it and expand it to other areas of your life.

Opportunities are all around to check in and see where you are and where you want to be. A situation reveals negativity and fear to be released and gifts and Light to be embraced and expanded. It can be a gauge to where you are in your growth and awareness. The more you are aware, the more this can work for you. Your level of awareness may ebb and flow at times. You may not be really aware all of the time and that's okay. You can wake up to a situation during the event or days, weeks, months, years later. There is no time requirement.

Be an observer of your life. Be aware, awake. Pay attention. Observe without attachment to what you see. Use this information to assess where you are, where you want to be. Your intuition will tell you what feels right to you at that time. Remember, if your heart feels light and free, you are in alignment with the person you truly are. If it feels heavy and tight, you may need to re-assess the situation. Trust yourself to know the difference. As you listen to your heart, it will speak to you more often and more loudly.

See your worth reflected in the world around you. Find where it is hiding from your view. Claim your gifts, purpose, truths, value, compassion and your ability to create what you want in life. See who you truly are inside and who you can become. Search for the you that you truly are for it will remain undiscovered until you choose to seek it.

There is a popular quote from Mahatma Gandhi: "You must be the change you wish to see in the world." I would suggest also that you must be the change you wish to see in your LIFE. You have the power. You are your own teacher.

We bring everyone into our lives to teach us. Those who come obviously as teachers don't necessarily know more than you. They have already discovered some things in themselves that you wish to discover at that time. Otherwise, you wouldn't have brought them into your life. They mirror back to you that which you want to discover— to remember who you truly are.

Shari and her ex-husband, Bill, had a challenging relationship. Every conversation they had was combative, stressful and argumentative. Shari believes that life is her mirror so she decided to experiment and change her actions in this situation. Before she was to talk to her ex-husband she centered herself, felt calm and opened her heart. She refused to be combative and she maintained calmness and a gentle tone throughout the conversation. As a result Bill remained calm and, for the first time, they didn't argue at all. He even commented that their conversation was more pleasant. Shari was thrilled that her experiment worked! From that point on Shari understood the mirror and used it to create more positive experiences throughout her life.

In some way, on some level, all of us have agreed to be mirrors to each other. It is a great gift we offer to one another. Welcome all of the teachers in your life and be grateful to yourself for placing them on your path. Observe what life mirrors and decide what you want to do with the information. It can be challenging to be comfortable with what you see in life's mirrors, especially the beauty in the mirror. The more you know who you are, the more you will understand your beauty.

One trick to remember if you feel stuck, stressed or anxious—laugh. Do whatever you need to do to laugh. Laughter shifts your mood instantly. It takes you out of the mire in a situation so you can see anything more clearly.

So, my friends, it's all about you. Express the gifts that are unique to you. Discover what you believe, not just what others believe, and make choices that reflect your beliefs.

Know you are lovable and valuable because you have true worth, not because another gives it to you. Forgive so you can have more compassion for yourself and then for others. Manifest what matters to you. Use life's mirrors so that you can know more of who you are and live the life you deserve.

Now that you have a better understanding of who you are and what you are doing here, create the life you want—a life full of happiness, joy, love, success or whatever you choose.

EXPLORATIONS

Think of a situation you recently experienced. Note how you reacted and responded to it. What kind of mood were you in? What thoughts went through your mind? What did you feel at the time?

Note what that situation could be telling you about yourself. What is it illuminating? Is it showing you fears and negativities to be addressed and released? Or possibly love, compassion, kindness or other aspects of yourself that you want to embrace and expand? Have the courage to see both.

If you didn't like the way the situation turned out, what can you do differently to change it? Could it be a different thought, word, action or a change in perspective?

If the situation turned out positively, where can you apply that positive aspect to other situations so they could be less challenging?

Once you understand how the mirror works, take it into daily life. Use life as your mirror and intuition as your guide.

Enjoy all of your explorations and expand your awareness every day of who you truly are.

NOTES

Exploring Your Potential...

101

About Julie

Julie Farha has a gift. As an Intuitive Facilitator, she helps people release blocks, align with their purposes and bring forth the joy and abundance waiting for them.

Julie has spent her life honing her natural intuitive skills and has developed a distinctive style of teaching and guiding. She has assisted private clients across the country and in Europe and is now sharing her talents with the public. Understanding that the path on which to reach a goal is as unique as the person seeking it, Julie emphasizes

103

the importance of discovering your true self. This is paramount to achieving what you desire in life.

Whether face to face or a continent away, Julie tunes in to each person's individual concerns and empowers him or her to map out a new way of responding to challenges in order to achieve lasting peace and satisfaction. Her formal education and training include a Bachelor of Arts degree from Arizona State University, Reiki certification and Life Coaching Fundamentals from the Southwest Institute of Healing Arts.

For multiple copy discounts and educational discounts

EVOLVING JOURNEYS PUBLISHING HOUSE

www.evolvingjourneys.com

Consultations

Keynote Speaker information

Seminars in your area

contact

author or publisher:

julie@clearinsightllc.com

www.clearinsightllc.com

EVOLVING JOURNEYS PUBLISHING HOUSE

www.evolvingjourneys.com